JOURNEYMAN'S
WAGES

JOURNEYMAN'S WAGES

CLEMENS STARCK

STORY LINE PRESS
1995

This publication was made possible by the generous support of the Nicholas Roerich Museum, the Andrew W. Mellon Foundation, and the National Endowment for the Arts, as well as our individual contributors.

ISBN: 1-885266-02-2

Book design by Joseph S. Bednarik

The cover shows a detail of a Chinese silk painting of the Tang Dynasty with the young Buddha practising archery. Musée Guimet, Paris.

Published by Story Line Press
Three Oaks Farm, Brownsville, Oregon 97327-9718

Library of Congress Cataloging-in-Publication Data

Starck, Clemens, 1937–
    Journeyman's wages / Clemens Starck.
        p.   cm.
    ISBN 1-885266-02-2
     1. Northwest, Pacific—Poetry.   I. Title.
PS3569.T33564J68   1995
811'.54—dc20   95-2465
                             CIP

ACKNOWLEDGMENTS

Some of these poems were first published in the following periodicals: *Calapooya Collage, Event, Fireweed, Hubbub, kayak, Labor Research Review, Left Bank, Longhouse, The Malahat Review, Mr. Cogito, On the Level, Split Shift,* and *Writing* (Vancouver, B.C.).

"Man Studying a Map" also appeared in the 1985 edition of *Anthology of Magazine Verse & Yearbook of American Poetry.*

"Me and Maloney" was reprinted in *Coffee Break Secrets: a cycle of poems about work,* selected and arranged for performance by Susan Eisenberg.

"Slab on Grade," "Me and Maloney," "Journeyman's Wages," "Dismantling," and "The Panama Canal" were anthologized in *Paperwork: Contemporary Poems from the Job,* edited by Tom Wayman.

"Slab on Grade" and "Me and Maloney" were included in *From Here We Speak: An Anthology of Oregon Poetry* (OSU Press: Oregon Literature Series).

Any acknowledgments would be incomplete without an expression of thanks to the many friends whose comments and suggestions over the years have helped significantly to fine-tune these poems and to inform this book.

This book
is addressed to
Les Compagnons du Devoir.

CONTENTS

I

II

III

IV

"It is true
that one kind of work is different from another;
but whoever carries out his duty impartially,
for him all work is equal."

—Meister Eckhart

I

"WILLAMETTE RIVER,
MARION ST. BRIDGE:
PIER 5, GENERAL DETAILS"

The sun slams into us
like one of the pile drivers
down on the gravel bar. The crew I'm on
is erecting forms for concrete piers.

Machinery roars. Earth shudders.
Cottonwood leaves turn gray with dust.

Companions of duty,
is this our assignment? Simply to be here, packed
in these heavy bodies, dumbfounded,
while time drags
and the river slides quietly by?

I signal the sun to slack off a little,
but nothing happens.
I keep on signaling anyway.

ME AND MALONEY

Job's nearly over,
me and Maloney all that's left of the crew.
Sunk in the hillside,
hundreds of tons of reinforced concrete
formed in the shape of a drum
ninety-two feet in diameter, eighteen feet deep—
it could be a kiva, or a hat box, or look from the air
like a missile silo.

It could be a storage tank for toxic waste.
It could be a vault to house
the national treasure.

In any case, it's finished,
ready for backfill. Now it's the earth's.

And I'm left with Maloney,
who likes to drink beer after work
and tell stories.
Construction stories. Ex-wife stories. Stories
like how he clubs possums to death with a two-by-four
when he finds them
prowling in back of his warehouse at night.

He laughs, telling the stories.

Maloney quit drinking once.
After a year and nine months he decided he'd rather
die of alcohol
than boredom.

4

I know what he means. I work
for Maloney Construction.
When it rains we work in the rain. When it snows
we work in the snow.
I am Maloney's right-hand man:
when he laughs I laugh too.

PUTTING IN FOOTINGS

Jake is the superintendent on this job,
I draw foreman's wages.
Mack the carpenter, Tom the laborer,
and there are others
wet to the skin
and cold to the bone—
that's Oregon in December.

Be joyful, my spirit. Be of high purpose.
We are putting in footings—
slogging through mud, kneeling
in it, supplicants pleading for mercy,
brutal, cursing,
drizzle coming down harder.

This is the Project Site.
Tobacco-chewing men in big machines dig holes,
we build the forms.
Ironworkers tie off rebar.
This concrete we pour could outlast
the Pyramids.

. . .

After the weather
has cleared, and the concrete has cured
and the paychecks are spent—

millennia later,
after the Pyramids
have pulverized and Jake has disappeared
and reappeared many times,
as grouchy as ever,
angels will come to measure our work,
slowly shaking their heads.

REMODELING THE HOUSE

The next step was
to tear out the dormer
some half-assed handyman cobbled together,
ruining the lines of this old house,
and build it back again
proper.

Now every true apprentice knows
there are principles to reckon with, spirit
level and plumb bob; so,
I honor the man who taught me
the soul is a house
and you build it,
                    joining the wood,
driving the nails home.

RAISING THE GRAIN

"The grain of rough lumber will show plainly in the finished concrete even though raising of grain is prevented by oiling the forms. If more pronounced grain marks are desired, the grain can be raised by wetting the lumber before oiling. A still more effective method is to spray the sheathing lumber with ammonia."

—*Forms for Architectural Concrete.*
Portland Cement Association, 1952.

1

The lot is vacant
except for me
and my tool box. My tool box
is huge
and is painted brown. It contains

little racks and holsters,
numerous compartments,
which hold all the tools I'll need for this job,
including a hacksaw.

What am I waiting for?

Everything is ready.

My chisels were dull, but for two hours
I've been sharpening them.

2

I am holding a hammer.
I am going to drive a nail.

But my hands, my hands are smashed
and bleeding!
The knuckles are raw.

It won't be easy—
it's never as easy as it looks . . .

—"What are you building, a piano?"

And when I have driven the nail
I am going to clinch it.

3

Already this year I've built
a Serbian Orthodox
Church,
and a mortuary
(Chapel of the Sunset, 26th Avenue
and Irving). Plus a number of other less tangible
structures.

My union dues are all paid up,
and I plan to continue
in the trade:
bookshelves for a crippled lady, a cage
for a boa constrictor . . .

The country is
going to hell, but a good mechanic
can always find work.

JOURNEYMAN'S WAGES

To the waters of the Willamette I come
in nearly perfect weather,
Monday morning
traffic backed up at the bridge
a bad sign.
        Be on the job at eight,
boots crunching in gravel;
cinch up the tool belt, string out the cords
to where we left off on Friday—
that stack of old
form lumber, that bucket of rusty bolts
and those two beat-up sawhorses
wait patiently for us.

Gil is still drunk, red-eyed, pretending he's not
and threatening to quit;
Gordon is studying the prints.
Slab on grade, tilt-up panels, Glu-lams
and trusses . . .

Boys, I've got an idea—
instead of a supermarket
why couldn't this be a cathedral?

JOB NO. 75–14

for Ron Boyce

Drive stakes, shoot grades,
get a big Cat to scalp and scrape and gouge:
contour the site for proper drainage.
Berm and swale.

Rough-grade it then, with
a blade, and hope
it don't rain. Set hubs,
haul in base rock, grade it again, then
pave it with a thick crust of blacktop
to make a parking lot.
                I'm building
a new Safeway, in West Salem,
for some religious millionaire,
and we will all buy our groceries there.

"Well, tomorrow's Friday," I say
to the guy who looks like Jesus driving stakes
and rod-hopping for me,
and he says "Yeah, then two!
and then five and then two and then five . . ."

Seven being a magic number
and the earth having a thin skin,
we make motions to bow
ceremoniously, but instead, a couple of
unmasked accomplices, confederates
on a losing planet,
we look at each other
and grin—
               which means: "to draw back the lips
so as to show the teeth
as a dog in snarling,
or a person in laughter or pain."

WHAT WE ARE DOING

What we are doing is hard to explain.
It would take diagrams and curse words, complicated
facial expressions
and lengthy descriptions of little-known tools. It would be
like trying to explain *quarks* and *leptons*
to someone who had merely asked
where the rest-rooms were.

However, to put it simply,
Davey and I
are on the fifth floor of the library, working
partners, jockeying stepladders
back and forth in the narrow aisles between the stacks,
not soaking up knowledge, but Pop-
riveting ceiling grid.

Davey has his ladder, I have mine; each
of us has a small vise-grips.
From Microbiology to Astrophysics,
dragging our tools and our bodies along with us,
we push on
inexorably, zigzagging
through the Dewey decimal system.

Pausing for a moment in Immunology,
naturally I think of Holub
peering into his microscope, making a poem
out of lymphocytes!
By the time we reach *The Bella Coola River Estuary*
and *Holocene Carbonate Sedimentation*,
it's noon, and time for lunch.

And cards! The game
has been going on for years,
at least since the time of the Pyramids, if not coeval
with carbonate sedimentation.
Five-card draw, jokers wild. We ante up . . .
Frank's three queens beat my two pair.
Davey's deal.

The afternoon will be a scorcher.

SLAB ON GRADE

At dawn the concrete trucks
are already there: revving their engines,
rumbling and throbbing, one by one
maneuvering into position.
Enormous insects,
on command
they ooze from their huge revolving abdomens
a thick gray slime.

Insects attending to insects,
the crew fusses over them, nursing wet concrete
into the forms.

Someone to handle the chute,
a couple laborers mucking, one pulling mesh, and two
finishers working the screed rod—
this is called pouring
slab on grade.

What could be flatter or more nondescript
than a concrete slab?
For years people will walk on it,
hardly considering that it was put there
on purpose,
on a Thursday in August
by men on their knees.

IN THE MEANTIME

Spiritual efforts may come to nothing;
right behavior's not easy to form.
In the workshop I put my tools in order
and sweep the floor—
sawdust and shavings, three bags full.

Idly I pick up a handsaw,
inspecting the blade for true.
This saw has a life, it uses my hands
for its own purpose. Lucky,
to know your own uses!

In the meantime I stay busy.
Emery cloth and steel wool
will take the rust off metal. Linseed oil
rubbed into the handles
keeps the wood alive.

THE CATHEDRAL

The decree was issued. A cathedral was to be built. *Ad majorem gloriam Dei,* etc. Workmen were chosen on the basis of their skill and their devotion to the Holy Faith. The foundations were laid, the walls begun. A scaffolding was erected, and tier by tier the great stones were set in place. As the walls rose, the scaffold rose alongside them.

Years passed. The structure was completed. Gargoyles, stained glass, flying buttresses—altogether an imposing achievement.

For centuries the stone nave absorbed the confessions of widows and murderers, followed by their urgent prayers for divine intercession. A plaster statue of the Virgin was said to have blushed once, and thus sanctity was embellished by a hint of the miraculous. The stoup for holy water, worn thin by daily usage, had to be replaced three times.

"Spiritual decay" (or an equally vague phrase) is the usual explanation for the rapid decline of the cathedral-building civilization. An exact chronology has never been fixed, but the already dilapidated cathedral was finally reduced to a pile of rubble. From time to time children playing among the stones discovered what later were determined to be religious artifacts. These were claimed by the authorities and removed to museums.

The site of the cathedral would long ago have been put to more productive use were it not for a singular phenomenon: towering above the ruins and completely encircling them, there remained the wooden scaffolding used by the original builders. This had never been torn down. It stands to this day, testimony to the marvelous wit and ingenuity of those ancient people.

II

UNLACING THE BOOTS

Unlacing my boots, I ease my feet into moccasins.
Soap and warm water absolve the skin from grime.
On the desk in my study are stacks of books—
ancient poems and other accounts
of men who lived on this planet once.
A good chunk of oak on the fire
will take the chill off my bones.

MAN STUDYING A MAP

There's a picture I have.
I've had it for years. My mother
had it before me.
An elderly English gentleman
in riding boots and scarlet jacket
sitting, knees apart,
on the edge of an old-fashioned horsehair couch.
Spread out on the floor in front of him
is a map at which he is pointing
with the tip of his long-stemmed pipe.
The room is dark
except for the glow from the fireplace
and light from a narrow window
high in the wall behind the couch.

I took him for my grandfather,
and always thought he must have been imprisoned there
in that dim room.
But now when I visit him he explains
there's no reason for me to be sad
for his sake. He has
all he needs: tobacco, couch, a crackling fire
and the map.

THE LAST EVENING

(Rainer Maria Rilke, *"Letzter Abend"*)

Night and the furthest distance; and the sword,
the army passing, at whose command they were . . .
He only glanced then from the harpsichord,
continuing to play, and looked at her

as in a mirror at himself: afraid
and unafraid, so flushed with youth, and knowing
no youthful promise could prevent his going,
sweet and seductive as the notes he played.

Then suddenly—as if the glass had broken!
She rose, about to speak, the words unspoken,
and heard the pounding of her heart instead.

His music died. Outside a breeze protested.
And motionless on the polished table rested
the stiff black shako with the white death's-head.

TWO CHINESE POETS

Mei Yaochen (1002–1058)

Mei Yaochen extolled the 'even and bland.'
His famous poem on the river-pig fish he wrote impromptu
after having dinner at Fan Zhongyan's.
Difficult scenes he could describe nonchalantly,
showing no signs of technical skill.
To aspiring poets who submitted their work
he would send a poem in reply.
For example,
in the one called "Reading
the Poetry Scroll of Magistrate Zhang" he says:
Although I have not allowed myself to become inattentive
          while reading them,
I cannot understand one out of ten!

Yang Wanli (1127–1206)

Yang Wanli was much praised
for his 'live method' of composition.
His friend Ge Tianmin wrote:
Yang understands how to make a dead snake leap with life.

Esteemed as one of the Four Masters etc.,
enlightened at 51,
he became even more matter-of-fact.
Regarding the immortal Li Bai's celebrated observation
          that Jade Mountain
falls over by itself without anyone pushing,
he said flatly: *Who gives a damn*
whether Jade Mountain falls over or not?

READING THE GOSPELS
IN THE LEE HOTEL

1

"Panorama Land" the tourist folders
call this place: the country hereabouts
unfolds, range after snowy range
in all directions,
and after that, clouds.

According to the account of what happened
as narrated by John,
in this translation,
Jesus said,
            "I came into this world
so that people might be set asunder,
so that those who cannot see should see,
and those who can see
should become blind."

2

I came here looking for a place to settle,
hopeful this might be it
this time,
            traveling from a distant constellation
to be here in this room, a newcomer
strange to the local customs.

And so it was. I was reading *The Four Gospels*,
listening to music through the static
on a San Francisco station . . .

Wallpaper peeling, woodwork encrusted with paint,
one bare light bulb dangling
by its wires from the high ceiling . . .
End of the line
for lonesome travelers, down and out.
One flight up, over the bar.
Lee Hotel.
   A drunk lurches, singing,
down the hall—body
trying clumsily to follow
the moves its spirit makes.
The radiator hisses.

"For judgment
I am come into this world" is how
the King James Version renders the passage.

   4

After midnight I go out,
bundled in checkered mackinaw and wool watch cap,
to walk the icy Main Street—
four blocks up, and five blocks back
on the other side, to an all-night café.

"Cheeseburger and coffee," I say
to the faded waitress.
     She's new in town herself,
she says, moving with accomplished
grace behind the counter
toward the stainless steel coffee urn.

THE ABANDONED
WACONDA RAILROAD STATION

No roof left at all, stone walls
dilapidated, blackberries creeping through
the empty windows—
it looks like one of those engravings
in an old book, of a ruined Roman villa,
or rather, an Eighteenth Century
English landscape architect's idea
of a ruined Roman villa;

that is, if in your mind
you can mask out
the thick stand of second- or third-growth
Douglas fir, and the ghosts of wistful travelers
still standing in line
to buy a one-way ticket to Portland.

RAILROAD CROSSING

Just turned twenty,
riding the freights through Oregon . . .
Came this way once, on these same tracks, lounging
in the doorway of an empty boxcar
rolling a cigarette,
waving nonchalantly at people in cars.

Twenty years later,
at the grade crossing on State Street, in Salem,
I squint impatiently into the afternoon sun,
engine idling,
waiting for a train to pass.

TUNED IN

The News is between 94 and 92
on my radio dial. I listen to it every
evening, I like
to keep informed.
In the morning I listen to it again,
the same News, re-broadcast.
I have a tape recorder, and I record the News,
play it back
at odd hours of the day,
and at night when I can't sleep.
People call, ask me
what I've been doing. I say
"I've been listening to the News."
Of course it's not always so easy. My dial
needs constant adjustment.
For whole days I get nothing but static,
and I think
it's the universe crackling.
But when I'm tuned in, I'm happy.
I listen
impassively—I know how important it is
to remain calm.
                    Even so, even so,
I nearly have an orgasm
every time a junta is overthrown.
I hate juntas.

Who do they think they're kidding?

Not me! I never
go out of the house—I don't have to.
There are maps tacked to my walls,
and I know
what's happening, everywhere.

OUT OF MY HEAD

I have a head, a noble
little skull.
Of all my possessions I love it the most.
More than my books or my bolo knife,
more than my tools,
more, even, than my entire collection
of petrified wood.

It's not in A-1 condition—the teeth
are rotten, the skin's a little tight
across the forehead—
but it's mine,
and I'm not complaining.

My head is my friend:
it talks to me,
it tells me what I want to hear.

Sometimes we go on trips together,
and it's fun.

It used to be different.
I lived in it then, like an animal
huddled in a cave.
But sooner or later you have to come out.
I don't know why.
Because you do, because you do . . .

So I did, and now I'm out.

I can do anything now, I'm free
to go anywhere. But whatever I do,
wherever I go,
I carry my head in my hands.

REGARDING THE ECLIPSE

Chances are I'll never tell
the story of how I found myself
adrift at sea
in a twelve-foot dinghy with a single oar;
or how, once, in the mountains
called Sierra Nevada,
trapped on a snowbound freight train,
my intrepid companions and I
existed for several days
on a fifty-pound sack of frozen marshmallows.

In retrospect
you could call it adventure, but at the time
it was nothing special. Anyway,
some events—like cloud formations
or teenage children—
are completely inexplicable.

My ambitions were nebulous at best.
All I ever wanted to be was a glass blower
or a wood carver,
or failing that, a utility infielder.
A career in the Foreign Service
looked promising once, but I couldn't feature myself
in formal attire
on a balcony overlooking the capital . . .
What would I be doing there?
Serving cocktails
to the Peruvian attaché's voluptuous wife?

And so it is that I stand
on the sagging porch of a tumbledown house
regarding the lunar eclipse
through binoculars held steady by my stalwart left hand.
With the other I gesticulate wildly,
but fail to observe
any change
in the shadow cast by this earth on the moon.

ADMIRING THE VIEW

Hummingbirds live in the thicket.
So do blackberries, roses, and flowering quince.
Just after sunrise the birds dart out,
buzzing and flashing
like tiny machines.

Like soap flakes
white rose petals melt on the lawn.
Minutes pass . . . Then hours, days, years.
When visitors come they admire the view.
I don't disagree.

Green hills. Blue sky. No clouds.

On the ridge to the east a hillside
has been logged off. Out over the valley
vultures circle,
soaring, riding the updrafts,
adjusting their great wings.

THROUGH THE HAZE

Old stories, poems, the dictionary—
sure, I read books,
but forget what I read, so what good does it do?
Studying, musing, staying up half the night . . .
Some say it's worthwhile, but it may
just be odd.

Alone for the day in an empty house.
Hot afternoon. I fall asleep . . .
and wake up with a headache, flies still buzzing, the
        evening sky
suffused with an eery yellow light.
The haze is so thick the hills are dim.
Things I was going to do I didn't do.
Four hours blank.

Fumbling for consciousness,
half-disbelieving the clock—how remote
it all seems now,
the lure of literature, and the singular hope
that words will clarify my life.

MOTHS

In the pump house where I go
to escape the TV
and the savagery of family life,
I share a light bulb with the moths.
They flutter. I read.

Or vice versa: they
are studying the light. That fierce white incandescence
interests them.
My blue eyes flutter across the page
like two pale moths.

When it's working right the pump cuts in
at 20 p.s.i.
          Meanwhile, I try
to pronounce correctly
the names, in Chinese, of the Five Classics.

The moths are excited. Moth dust
settles impalpably
in the forest of hair on the back of my hand.

At 40 the pump cuts out. Now
I can hear myself talking—but still
can't quite tell
what it is that is being said.

LOOKING FOR PARTS

1

Leaning on the counter of the local
auto parts store,
a man is telling a story
about a clutch.

What *I'm* after is a left front
shock absorber bracket
for my pickup. He's only looking
for conversation.

He looks like Humphrey Bogart
with a blotchy face. I probably
look odd myself.

"Those old Chevies were good trucks,"
we agree. Our lives
are linked by machines.

2

They don't have the part,
but I get one from the wrecker:
left hand gloved in leather
to hold the cold-chisel, right hand brandishing
a maul . . .
                    Down on one knee in the weeds,
bent over a wrecked truck chassis,
I notice the ground is soaked
with crankcase oil
and littered with nuts and bolts.

Straightening up, I can see
a black dog chained

to an old yellow schoolbus. Acres of scrapmetal
flaking with rust.
A goldfinch flits through a thistle patch.

                    3

A plywood and tarpaper shack
has *OFFiCE* lettered crudely over the door.
Inside, a counter
unbelievably cluttered, a miniature junkyard
behind which the burly proprietor sits,
an immortal in greasy coveralls
chewing on a cigar. He says
he sold his yard in Junction City
to buy this one.
                    Over his pocket, stitched in red,
is the one word: *Jim*.

                    4

Directly behind the stitching
in the chamber formed by a cage of bone
is the man's heart.
I hand him three dollars
and climb in my truck.
                    It's not fog
that reduces visibility now,
but streams of white fluff blown by the wind—
a snowstorm in August, each flake
a whole galaxy.
Thistledown! thistledown!

Mulling this over, I cruise down the highway.
Hands rest lightly on the wheel.
Oil changed, new plugs and points—pickup
running like a charm.

A SUNDAY DRIVE

The highway out of Salem
crosses the Willamette and skirts the Eola Hills.
It goes to the coast,
a foot-thick, forty-foot-wide asphalt strap
edged with gravel, weeds
and the bodies of small animals.
In places the earth has been gouged
to receive it.

On Sundays people go for a drive.
Following the signs for Ocean Beaches, an hour or so,
in no time they're there.
Park. Get out and stretch
and walk for awhile,
leaving shoe-prints in the wet sand.
Later the kids want to stop for pizza.

If it's autumn, the drive home will be spectacular.
Fog settles in the hollows.
Woodsmoke merges with the fog.
Mountains of shaggy green-black fir forest
set off the hardwoods—
maples' fiery yellow,
oak leaves touched with rust.

BUTCHERING RABBITS

To kill one with a single blow takes force.
It leaves them limp, stretched out in the grass
without a tremor,
white and black and reddish-brown,
a trickle of blood from the nostrils—
nameless *things*, that used to be called
Ginger, Popcorn, Snowball, Liz . . .

Skin clings tenaciously to the carcass;
flesh is soft but hard to carve.
My knives are sharp, but unlike Cook Ding
my skill is slight.

Fortunately my wife will transform all this
death to some purpose.
Her rabbit stew is incomparable.

SNOWDROPS

In February my children pick snowdrops
and put them to float in a dish of water. Small
white petals streaked with green,
you are like my children, floating,
floating on clear water.

CUTTING THE GRASS

When the power mower quits
I pick up the scythe
and attack the vegetation like a storm-trooper,
cutting a swath in the overgrown yard.
My children rake and fork it into piles,
not without grumbling a little,
but mildly.

All afternoon, with breaks for lemonade,
we give the place a haircut.
Grass piles multiply.
Hollows and hummocks appear.
Avoiding his shadow
the black cat steps gingerly through the stubble.
A single yellowjacket mirrors
what's left of the sun.

My father had a scythe
identical to this one: standing there, wiping his brow
with a white handkerchief.

Come closer, children,
this is the Kingdom of Heaven.
Look.
     (I should mention also,
sweet as it was,
for dessert that night we had chocolate pudding.)

AN INVITATION

Friends, if you'll stop by sometime
I'll take off this serious face.
We'll smoke
and get into some blackberry wine—
this year's batch
is just right!
          My old neighbor the moon
will climb out of the hills,
happy to join us.
Yardlights a mile away in the valley
will be no closer
than the nearest star.

Half-lit ourselves, we'll sit
on the veranda
telling preposterous stories.
Like the one that begins:
               "Long ago
on this planet there was a man,
an ordinary man . . ."

A country place is quiet at night.
In the woods sometimes an owl,
or coyotes—upstairs,
one of the kids must be having a dream.

PRACTISING ARCHERY

Mist in the firs. Moss on the oaks.
The weather, this time of year, is impossible.
Snow on the mountains—no,
those are clouds!

Two little Chinamen, kneeling,
one is in brick-colored pajamas, the other
in charcoal-colored pajamas, each
drawing a bow . . .
                What's this all about,
the young Buddha practising archery?

Everywhere dark firs
stick straight up
through lighter moss-green oaks. White
patches of mist float down the hillsides
from higher elevations.
Oregon is not so far from China.

The archers kneel, their bows pulled taut.
Their aim is true. There are no arrows
fitted to the string.
There is little, really, to worry about,
but I still do.

IV

VI

CHRYSANTHEMUMS

Yellow and orange, so heavy with rain
they have to be tied in bunches and fastened
by baling twine
to the side of the shed. And mistletoe,
dark knots of it visible now
high in the bare oaks. Underfoot,
a mattress of soggy leaves.

On my birthday I get up early,
stirred by a vague excitement.
"It's snowing, it's snowing!" the children sing out.
First snow of the year.

Approaching fifty a man starts
counting backwards.
After driving the kids to school in town
I stop for gas. While Stu fixes
the loose windshield wiper
we touch on lung cancer, carburetor trouble,
this thing and that.

THE PANAMA CANAL

My neighbor, an out-of-work welder,
is of the opinion that—well, you take for example
the Panama Canal . . .
"It was ours!" he keeps saying.
"It was built with our own sweat and blood!"

He would never have given it away
as our spineless President did.

All week it's been raining.
Jobs are scarce and he's been laid off.
However, he believes
the new President, a hard-liner,
will get this country back where it should be.

"Of course," he concedes
with a boyish grin, "there might be war."
But he doesn't think the Russians
will put up much of a fight.

While we talk, I can hear his wife
inside, vacuuming.

WHY WE ARE AFRAID

My family is bored. We have everything.
There's nothing left for us to have, except maybe
a space shuttle
or an automatic ice-cube maker.
Verily, merchandise breeds merchandise.
Every day new catalogues arrive.
But it's no use. Whatever they're selling
we've already got.

My country, too, is bored. Even more so, because
it has the space shuttle
and it can make ice cubes at a prodigious rate.
And that is why we're so afraid,
and why we need
bombers that can fly through the eye of a needle,
bullets that travel backwards and forwards,
crossbows
and harquebuses
to protect us from our enemies.

What I say, is: Enemies, when you arrive
you can have it all! I'll leave
instructions for the microwave
next to the sink in the bottom drawer.

HONOLULU

It was all new to me!
When the crew messman went berserk
we were three days at sea,
Long Beach
to Yokosuka on an MSTS charter.

First we had to catch him—he was fast
and crazy. Then
he was strait-jacketed, sedated, and chained
to a bunk in the ship's infirmary.

Under new orders
we changed course, steamed north
for Honolulu; docked
two days later,
put him off, and took on bunkers there.

That night, standing gangway watch,
the warm Hawaiian air
redolent with the smell of diesel fuel,
I thought of the crew messman.

Both his arms were covered with tattoos—
dragons and roses,
names of women,
elaborate patterns of blue
and red.

AMMO SHIP

Mostly we hauled asphalt,
tens of thousands of drums of asphalt.
The master-plan
called for southeast Asia to be a parking lot.
If it wasn't asphalt, it was bombs.
The bombs were for the enemy.

One trip, four days out of southern California
in heavy seas, the cargo began to shift.
We climbed down into the hold with shoring timbers
        and wedges.
The bombs in their fragile wooden crates
tossed about like restless sleepers,
a nightmare screech of nails pulling and wood
splintering.
                The rest of the trip
morale was low. Not even
the cook's special blueberry pancakes
helped.

The people the bombs were for
scattered. Deer at the start of hunting season,
they knew we were coming
and they were scared too.

OREGON THREE TIMES

1

The first time was on a freight train
from Utah. (I was headed for Kansas City,
but got turned around.)
At Klamath Falls a railroad dick
probed the boxcar with a flashlight:
"Any coons in there?"

2

The second time I had a wife
and an old Buick.
We drove up from California.
For recreation I bought a fishing rod and reel
at a sporting goods store in Springfield.
I've still got the reel.

3

The third time: a merchant ship
just in from the Far East.
Longshoremen loaded us with lumber at Newport
in the rain.
We all went into town. Got drunk.
It was our own country.

COMMUTING

Firs on the hillside:
mist drifts through them like smoke.
White mist, black trees . . .
Headlights sweep the wet pavement.
Waiting at home
my son—he's ten, he wants to know
what we're here for.
Black firs. White mist.
Loose tools rattle in the back of the truck.
In twenty miles I ought to be able
to figure out something.

CHANGING THE ALTERNATOR BELT
ON YOUR 504

1

To do this the radiator
must be removed. Two bolts on top, three
on the bottom, and disconnect
the hoses.
Four small screws, and the shroud
comes loose. This leaves
the radiator free.

Lift it out carefully. Set it
outside the garage, on the gravel.
Take five.
Smoke.
Contemplate the plum tree.

2

If the soul took shape
it might look like that—a cloud of white blossoms
throbbing with bees . . .
In the rank grass,
daffodils flaunt their yellow message.
Six fat robins
skitter across the pasture.

It makes no sense.
Eddie Rodriguez is dying. You know
that you are dying too,
and still there is spring
and fixing cars.

3

With the radiator out,
the rest is easy.
After replacing the belt, reverse the procedure:
radiator, hoses, anti-freeze.

Turn on the ignition.
Be brave. Be sad. Check for leaks.
Wipe your greasy hands on a rag.
Drive on,
brother, drive on.

for E.R., 1945–1987

POEM WRITTEN IN THE PARKING LOT
OF A SEVEN-ELEVEN

No breeze to ruffle the maple leaves.
The hills at the edge of town
are brown. Toy cars
slide up to the Seven-Eleven,
and stop. A delivery van is delivering
video games.

Also to be observed
are the conformation of clouds, the proximity
of mountains,
and the absence of gunfire.

On their way home from school
children loiter,
sucking refreshment from large paper cups
that say *Pepsi*—
white, red, and blue.

        . . .

The afternoon
develops slowly. Every so often,
agitated by passing traffic,
a scrap of paper
drifts to the west, and then to the east.

Like answers to irrelevant questions,
a few blocks away, gathering speed,
trucks hurtle by
on their way out of town.

HOW IT WILL BE

Heavy rains. The river swollen.
Soldiers in rubber rafts. On the bank, a horse's
bloated carcass,
and the sprawled remains
of those who manned a machine-gun nest.

Wartime photograph.
Caption reads: "Partisans crossing the Drina,
May 1943."

One of the soldiers looks like my uncle.
Rifle slung over his shoulder, he is reciting
the Ten Commandments,
or else he is telling the others
how it will be
after the war.

Are they advancing, or retreating?
Is there hope? or is this desperation?
Nothing is clear.
Gray skies. The water muddy.
In the Book of Paradise it is written:
"Brothers! Sisters! How many rivers must we cross
before the final victory?"

One of my uncles *was* a soldier—
Fort Benning, Georgia . . . Germany . . . then Japan.
Another preached the word of God.
The third was a janitor.

FALLING OFF THE ROOF, I MISS
THE FALLS CITY FOURTH OF JULY
PARADE AND PICNIC

X-rays negative, I limp across the parking lot.
Driving home I remember my father telling
how my grandfather used to make a patriotic speech
to his congregation
every year on the Fourth.
Later I learn that my elder daughter
came in second in the sack race.

IN THE MIDDLE OF THE NIGHT, WAKING FROM A DREAM OF MY CHILDREN, I GO DOWNSTAIRS AND READ DU FU

Troubles erupt—like a skin rash.
Worry gnaws at the innards, a belligerent
ulcer.
        In twelve hundred years
no parent has ever
found a solution for this.

I stoke the fire. Smoke
sucked up the chimney
resembles a prayer or a curse.
Spurned by forty publishers, my poems
go unread.

So is it any wonder
that the doctor says "You'll be taking these pills
for the rest of your life"?

DISMANTLING

Call Joel (eves) 623-9765

Smack in the public eye
at Ninth and Van Buren, tearing down
an old house—
"Not demolition, dismantling!" says Joel. Slowly
we make the house disappear.
It takes a few months.
We do this for a living.
               Our sign says:
USED LUMBER FOR SALE.
Neat stacks of it on the front lawn
around a dormant forsythia—
shiplap and siding, and over here
we have two-by . . .
That pile is already sold.

We also have toilets, sinks, remarkable
savings on bent nails,
French doors, free kindling
and more. Lots more.

         . . .

With the roof off
a house looks more like a cathedral,
rafters outlined against the sky.
A pair of ragged priests,
stick by stick we celebrate
nothing. We are making the shape of nothing,
creating
an absence.

And when we have finished,
what will there be at Ninth and Van Buren?
A square of bare earth
where a house was.
Sidewalk. Foundation. Concrete stoop.
Two steps up
and you're there.

NOTES

"WILLAMETTE RIVER, MARION ST. BRIDGE...": The name of the river and the valley in western Oregon is pronounced to rhyme with *Damn it!* Thus: wil-LAM-mit.

WHAT WE ARE DOING: Miroslav Holub (1923–) is the eminent Czech poet also renowned for his work as a scientist in the field of immunology.

READING THE GOSPELS IN THE LEE HOTEL: The rendition of John ix:39 is from E.V. Rieu's translation, *The Four Gospels*, in the Penguin Classics.

TWO CHINESE POETS: These sketches are drawn from material contained in Jonathan Chaves' *Mei Yao-ch'en and the Development of Early Sung Poetry* and J.D. Schmidt's *Yang Wan-li*. Chaves' translations of Yang—*Heaven My Blanket, Earth My Pillow*—are also to be enthusiastically recommended.

Li Bai = Li Po (701–762). He was already in Yang's time a legendary figure.

BUTCHERING RABBITS: Cook Ding is a master butcher mentioned in the *Zhuangzi*. So phenomenal is his skill, so attuned is he to the Dao, that despite his having carved up thousands of oxen over a period of nineteen years, he has never had to sharpen his knife.

HONOLULU: During wartime the Military Sea Transportation Service (MSTS), a branch of the U.S. Navy, contracted with private steamship companies for transport of war matériel.

CHANGING THE ALTERNATOR BELT ON YOUR 504: That is, on your Peugeot 504. The 'Five-oh-four' was the car model manufactured by the French auto-maker during the 1970s.

IN THE MIDDLE OF THE NIGHT... : Du Fu = Tu Fu (712–770).

CLEMENS STARCK has worked as a merchant seaman, a reporter on Wall Street, a ranch hand, and a construction foreman. Presently he earns his living as a journeyman carpenter at Oregon State University. Starck's poetry has appeared in a wide variety of publications, including the anthologies *From Here We Speak: An Anthology of Oregon Poetry* and *Paperwork: Contemporary Poems from the Job.* He lives in rural Oregon.

The text of this book is set in 11 pt. Times Roman. Created by Stanley Morison for *The Times* of London in 1931 and based on the old-style Dutch type Plantin, the design provided the newspaper with a type that conserved space yet appeared large, highly legible, and rather strong in weight. A workhorse among types, it is notable for its dignity and clarity when set large, and for its almost miraculously high legibility in the smallest settings.